IT'S ALL FUCKING POSSIBLE

YOUR GUIDE TO OVERCOMING AN 'IMPOSSIBLE' GOAL

SARAH QUINN

RED THREAD PUBLISHING

Red Thread Publishing LLC. 2021

Write to info@redthreadbooks.com if you are interested in publishing with Red Thread Publishing. Learn more about publications or foreign rights acquisitions of our catalog of books: www.redthreadbooks.com

Paperback ISBN: 9781955683111

Ebook ISBN: 9781955683135

Rather than write a formal dedication. I want you to take a moment right now, pause, breathe in and notice who you are. How you are. Be present to all that has happened to you. Be present to all that is currently happening within you, around you and outside of you.

Thank this person you are right now for all he or she has been. When you do the work in this book you will grow, your life will change. Decide what you want to hold onto and bring it forward. Decide what you can let go of and thank it for all it's done for you.

Breathe in gratitude and exhale to set it all free.
Let's begin

CONTENTS

Introduction vii

1. Everything Is Possible 1
2. The Rule 6
3. It's Time to Set Your Goal 7
4. It`s All Fucking Possible 9
5. I Saw the Sign 13
6. It's YOU vs. YOU 15
7. It's Time to Just Show the Fuck Up 18
8. Thinking About Changing Your Goal? 20
9. Having It All 22
10. Creating Certainty 26
11. The Marketing Side of Achieving Your Goal 28
12. Cleaning Up Your Workspace 32
13. Do Whatever Is Necessary To Bring Your Ideas To Life 34
14. The Kick in The Ass You Need 36
15. A Mindset Hack To Help You Stretch 38
16. Time 40
17. Managing your time to Support Your Impossible Goal 42
18. Money Talk 45

A Note from Me 47

Thank you 51

Also by Sarah Quinn: Have It All 53

100-Day Journal Prompts For Ready to Be 6 & 7 Figure Coaches 57

Coded For Money, Flow and Fame 61

About the Author 63

About Red Thread Publishing 65

Also by Red Thread Publishing 67

INTRODUCTION

An Impossible Goal has the word possible in it. That tells you everything you need to know. Here's the thing. I don't believe you or I have limits as to what we can create in this life because everything is possible.

The question is, why haven't you truly created the version of your life or business that excites you?

Everything is possible. Let's get that straight right now because this book isn't about convincing you that your big-ass dreams are out there for you to achieve. It's about pushing you to your limits so you DO achieve them.

Hopefully, by now you've had a chance to dive into the first three books in the Quit Fucking Around series. For those that have, you have a MAJOR advantage because you are likely already dreaming big and taking bold actions in your life. If not, no worries. I'm going to kick your ass into shape the Sarah Quinn way.

Let's take a look at what I mean when I say everything is possible.

Humanity has just begun uncovering the wonders of the world and its capabilities. What has been labeled as leaps and bounds in worldly development over the last decade is nothing compared to what's to come.

With each new advancement comes multiple opportunities.

Think of it as a tomato plant (I know, weird, but, stick with me) what starts out as a seed becomes a plant producing luscious red fruit, right? Or is that all?

When I look at that seed, I see fields, a farmer, and workers. I also see trucks that transport the goods, vegetable stands on the side of the road; tomato sauce on a grocery shelf, and bruschetta bread at my favorite restaurants.

I see agriculture, jobs, food, memories around a table, and global connection points bringing people and companies together.

The growth of a single seed has so much potential, and so do you, my Luv.

In this book, you are the tiny little seed buried underground and I'm about to dose you with some water and sunlight, and a dash of organic fertilizer, and we're going to see just how big you can grow, and how far you can go.

1
EVERYTHING IS POSSIBLE

As I said, everything is possible, you, my friend have come up with 51 shades of crazy-ass reasons why it isn't.

The impossible goal is quite simple to understand. It's a goal that your mind doesn't perceive as possible…yet. The keyword here is YET.

As a business coach, I've heard 'but how', more times than I can count. This 'but how' gets transferred into an excuse not to do anything.

Some of the excuses below may sound familiar:

- I'm not in alignment
- I need to find my passion
- I don't see how I'm going to overcome X
- I just need to get motivated
- I'm such a procrastinator, perfectionist, bad at sales, and so on.

Those excuses may turn into 'I don't really know what I want, so I'm not going to get anything done until I figure THAT out.' Sadly, and

I hate to burst your oh-so-glamorous shades of crazy, but the truth is you DO know what you want and you do know how to get it.

You want love, friendship, connection, security, wealth, safety, excitement, growth and, and, and. Who doesn't want that stuff? Can you honestly tell me you don't want any of these things? You may want some more than others, or you may value one over the other, but at the end of the day, you want happiness. Happiness comes from love, friendship, connection, and, and, and.

We experience these feelings and achievements through various outlets. Love, especially self-love, gives you comfort, and comfort gives you some degree of happiness. If you disagree, think about the last time you had to pee REALLY bad and you were stuck in traffic and had to hold it. Talk about discomfort...I'll bet you let out a deep sigh of relief and a 'thank goodness' when you were done tinkling.

When you have enough to pay your bills you feel secure and security brings you happiness.

When you don't have money to pay for your basic needs tell me how happy you feel? But Sarah… (shaking my head because there is always one of you with that damn 'but' word) if I had more money, I'd be happier. Perhaps that is true for you, yet happy is happy. Happier is a variation of happiness. You can have more or less and you are still experiencing happiness.

So you see, you DO know what you want and as I said, you're stuck on the HOW.

- How do I have self-love?
- How do I have more money?
- How do I… (insert any reason you've currently found to be 'unhappy')?
- How do I find someone to love me?
- I'm flat broke, how do I pay my bills?

You already know the answer to all of this too!

. . .

I'm going to be a little bit bold here and call you a liar. I know you are because we all are. Even though I practice what I teach, I am too sometimes. There is always that one lie that creeps through when I least expect it and it hinders me from having what I really want.

If you're flat broke and this feels true for you, I want to invite you to look at this a little differently.

Look down at your hands right now. Seriously look at them. You are reading this book either on some form of device, or the physical book is in your hands, which means money bought it, and if you bought it you had some amount of money and you aren't flat broke.

Flat broke means nothing in the bank and nothing coming in…at all...ever. I presume that's probably not the case for most or all of you. Uncertain as to how you're going to pay rent may be the more probable statement.

Right there is proof that if you are walking around saying I'm flat broke or some other variation of that, it's a lie. If you're saying something like I don't have money, how am I going to pay my bills...well, you know the answer to that too.

- Get up off your butt and fill out every application until you get a job.
- Go to work, get a paycheck and pay your bills.
- Or put offers on the table in your business ALL DAY, EVERY DAY until someone buys, and then you do it again, and again and again.
- Or you rent out a room in your house.
- Or you sell your car and start walking.
- Or you get a loan.
- Or you move somewhere cheaper.

- Or.. or.. or I could go on and on.

You see, you can do all of these things or one of these things even, and voila! You have a solution. You can move to a cheaper apartment, get a part-time job, put 20 offers a day out on your lunch break, sell your car, pay off some debt, walk and get healthy, and now you're rocking!

It's called an impossible goal because most people don't see solutions this way. Most people will hold onto their problems and stay stuck, wait for someone else to fix them, or slap a band-aid solution on it. When that band-aid falls off they wonder why the hell they are still dealing with this problem.

I'll break this down nicely and simply. The impossible goal is a goal that is so big and so far out there that your brain truly cannot comprehend how you will achieve it; therefore, you believe it's impossible.

Let's reframe that and from here on out we are calling it the possibly impossible goal. If you look at it the right way and ask the right questions or make the right choices, you may achieve it. The possibly impossible goal is designed to make you fail forward over and over and over until you grow into the person who can see exactly how to achieve it.

Every year on New Year's Eve I set a possibly impossible goal. I then spend 365 days learning who I can grow into and just how far I can reach toward achieving it.

I won't sugarcoat it. It's not like taking a walk on a beautiful sunny day with a perfect breeze and a chai tea latte in your hands. It's more like running shoes with no socks in the winter in 6 feet of snow.

. . .

Imagine the glory of that beautiful sunny day. You feel good, yet if you stuck it out, you'd also feel good once you trekked through the snow and finally made it to your nice warm home. Only in this scenario will your legs get stronger from the exercise AND that hot cup of cocoa feels divine as it warms your body.

The journey may be tougher, yet the rewards are greater. Now that you've made it through the trek in the snow, you can certainly take on that 10k Spartan race you're avoiding!

Oops, I'm talking about me here!

2

THE RULE

There is a rule that comes with an impossible goal. You must follow this rule every step of the way. No matter what. You cannot alter this rule. You cannot bend it. You cannot break it.

This is your only rule: You cannot change your impossible goal in any way.

3

IT'S TIME TO SET YOUR GOAL

Every coach I've ever worked with has told me, "Dream big, Sarah." When I set a goal, they immediately raise their eyebrows and say maybe we should start smaller.

Ummm nope! I'm gonna start here nice and BIG!

By setting a massive goal, even if I 'fail' I've still achieved something I probably never would have with a smaller goal. I'm setting myself up to grow into the kind of person who can achieve anything.

This year's goal has been to create a world-class life while having both of my companies bring in $300k each month. Oh hello, Covid! You've come to make my seemingly impossible goal REALLY difficult.

My first step was to determine what world-class means to me, and then by habit, I jumped right into how the hell am I going to make $600k a month?

That's the thought that people go to every single time. I'll get to the how part in the next chapters, but for now, I want you to dream big. REALLY BIG!

. . .

What is your impossible goal? Remember, you are setting this goal for one year.

Don't let the time frame limit your ability to dream big, let it be a boundary that you know you will push through and achieve in one year. When you achieve that goal, you have achieved the seemingly impossible.

Here are some goals my clients have set for themselves:

- *"I want to grow my community to 10,000 women who are all actively participating in at least one of my programs. -Lacey" Lacey started out with 47 members in her community that were paid clients and an email list of 124 subscribers that she had not emailed in at least 5 months.*
- *"I want to speak on 6 stages a month and get paid for every one of them. -Tina"*
- *"I'm making $2000 a month now. I want to make one million dollars each quarter. -Zach"*
- *"I want to become a billionaire. -Mark"*
- *"I want to have 20 rental properties. -Aleasha"*

4

IT`S ALL FUCKING POSSIBLE

You just set a crazy big goal. How do you feel?

I remember the first time I set an impossible goal. I felt so dang excited and approximately 3 hours later, I had already found a dozen reasons why I couldn't, shouldn't, and wouldn't achieve it.

Over the years I've run a year-long support group for entrepreneurs who want to achieve massive growth. Let me tell you, last year 47 brave souls stepped into the arena, and today there are only 2 standing, one of them being myself. I want you to do better than that, so let's take a look at what type of things you're going to say:

I'm just going to give myself more time.

CHEATER! That's not how this works. You have 12 months, 52 weeks, 365 days, 8760 hours, 525,600 minutes. Do you mean to tell me, you don't trust yourself enough to learn how to get this done? I'm calling your bluff.

A 15-year-old boy worked his summer job and made $7000. He asked his parents what he was supposed to do with the money now that summer was over. His father, being somewhat savvy with stocks, decided to share some basic lessons with his growing teen. He gave his son some stock options that may be of interest to him. The boy chose to stick his money in a small roller skate company and by chance, that roller skate company grew and that boy now has $160,000.

You are probably thinking, that's just luck. WRONG! That's chance, and chance only happens when we step into it and take action. He took a chance and it paid off. So keep your timeline and fearlessly take as many chances as you need to, to achieve your goal.

It was unrealistic anyway.

What's your point? If I have to explain this one in detail, I want you to flip back to the beginning of the book and start over again. The impossible goal IS unrealistic. It IS unbelievable. It IS hard. Wait, it's not hard, it's simply not what you are used to.

You can get used to it. Just because something seems unrealistic doesn't mean it is; it means you THINK it is, but you can control your thoughts.

What if I just aim for X instead of Z?

No, no, no. Remember the ONE rule, you do not get to change your goal. Besides, do you think you can't achieve your goal? Dig down deep and ask yourself, can I do this? I know, that you know, that you can achieve your goal, and you're simply scared right now.

Being scared doesn't define can or can't; it defines will or won't. You can be scared and still do something anyway. The question is WILL YOU? I say yes, yes, you will show up for yourself, for your dreams, for your goals. I know if you've come this far, you have it in you.

It's just too hard.

You're right, it is damn hard, and that's exactly what is going to make the journey transformational. You'll get to discover what you've got in you. You'll get to discover what's on the other side of hard, and let me tell you, it's friggin' amazing.

It's life-altering amazing. It's when you've dug deep inside of yourself and finally found yourself buried underneath everything the world has thrown at you since day one. So embrace the hard. Learn to love the hard and get excited when things challenge you. All it means is that you are growing.

My friends, family, and/or partner just don't understand.

Isn't it damn infuriating when the people you love the most suddenly don't seem to *get you*? When you feel as though you're outgrowing everyone around you, what do you do? When you suddenly try to make yourself smaller to keep things the same, what are you doing?

Do you REALLY want to stay the same?

Do you want to be small?

Do you want to be less than you were meant to be?

Do you want to experience all that you can be and trust that true happiness lies in being fully and authentically you?

When the naysayers start talking, I go into tunnel vision, with full focus on who I am meant to be. I let the rest fall where it's meant to. It's not easy, and it doesn't always feel good, but I know with 100% certainty that the people around me love and value me for me.

I don't know where the money is going to come from.

Really? When you claim what you want and claim that it's the only level you will live at, play at, and dream of, the world is going to GIVE IT TO YOU. JUST LIKE THAT! It will happen when you stop focusing on how and trust that the world WILL deliver. I know that's a big ask, but try it on for a while

Money should NEVER be the reason you don't chase your dreams, because where there is a will, there is a way.

. . .

I'm already behind where I need to be so I'll start over next year.

Did you hear me? What is the rule, the only damn rule? You cannot change, alter or adjust your impossible goal, which means you cannot change the timeline. You MUST keep going otherwise what you're saying is that it's ok with you to quit on yourself.

Let's be honest, you are worth it unless, of course, you are trying to say you aren't worth it in which case we have a lot of work to do. KEEP YOUR BUTT A'MOVING ...You've got this!

5
I SAW THE SIGN

How do I know if I'm getting there? I like to use a tool taken from my Life By Design Course (access life by design Resources free www.sarahquinncoaching.com/life-by-design-resources.)

I do this weekly and the reason for that is that I've given myself a mere 52 weeks to achieve my possibly impossible goal, so there isn't time to waste. It's simple. I take 12 different areas of life and I journal the following:

Health

What do I want to start believing?

- …expecting?
- …feeling?
- …valuing?
- …believing more of it?
- …expecting more of it?
- …feeling more of?
- …valuing more of?

- ...continue believing in?
- ...continue expecting?
- ...continue feeling?
- ...continue valuing?

I practice the same action steps for my intellect, emotions, character, spirituality, love relationships, parenting, social life, career, finance, life vision, and quality of life.

Next, I look for evidence of what I experienced the previous 7 days. Where is the proof that I started believing more of/in X?

If there's no proof and I haven't yet taken action on growing in a particular area, I identify a micro-shift that I can implement to create it. Maybe you are thinking, *'but these don't help the goal I set for myself.'* Shaking my head over here at you (with love, of course), I ask myself, "Are you really listening?"

The impossible goal is about growing into the kind of person who can figure out how to achieve it. Which means YOU NEED TO CHANGE.

Scratch that, you GET to change.

6

IT'S YOU VS. YOU

The possibly impossible goal is a game of you vs. you. I am extremely competitive so this is a really interesting space for me personally. To be honest, I think it gives me an advantage (don't let that discourage you if you aren't competitive, I've got a secret strategy for ya!)

The voice in my head is always competing for how we do it better, faster, with more ease, in a way that brings me more joy. I teach this in-depth in Life By Design, but let's touch on it here so you can get a grasp on how to compete with your own worst enemy- yourself.

What happens in your head as soon as you set any goal is that the fear trigger kicks in. You can recognize this happening when your inner voice starts saying things such as:

- How am I ever going to get to...
- I'll never be able to...
- Why on earth did I agree to this?
- It can't possibly be this hard.
- If only I had...
- And on and on and on.

So how does one compete against themselves? They stop pretending. Here is what I want you to do. I want you to stop pretending that:

- You are OK with an unhappy relationship.
- You are OK with little to no clients.
- You are OK with clients who don't pay on time.
- You are OK doing it all on your own.
- You are OK with boring and mundane conversations.
- It didn't matter, you didn't celebrate that amazing thing you achieved.
- You want to be around your kids 24/7 and your Pinterest pictures are actually how you live.
- Social media is the only way you can achieve success.
- Success looks like...
- You can be like someone else.
- Your $5000 a month sales are enough.
- It's OK if you put off that vacation.
- You don't have what it takes.
- There's more time and you can do it another day.
- Don't like it, don't do it. Don't want it, don't settle.
- Don't have time, don't say yes.
- If you hate commercials on YouTube, upgrade your account.
- If you want to dress sexy when everyone else is in sweats, DO IT.
- Can't stand that 'friend' who you keep putting up with, GET RID OF THEM.

Just stop fucking pretending.

BE.

Yes, BE. Just be, who and how you are! Something friggin' magical happens when you are true to yourself, everything just gets so damn easy and it feels SO good. You no longer have to compete with yourself when you just step into who you are, fully into who you are. No more hiding. No more guilt. No more shame.

. . .

Every time you say something and then you think, ugh, I should have said this instead, come out and say it.

Every time you say yes to something when it was meant to be no, apologize and let it be a no.

Notice when you feel uncomfortable, change it.

Notice when you quiet yourself, get loud.

Stop suppressing.

Stop ignoring.

Stop wishing.

Start doing.

Start being.

Start experiencing.

Start feeling all of the things you were meant to and you will just be you. You will no longer be in a war of you vs. you.

7

IT'S TIME TO JUST SHOW THE FUCK UP

You are here because you are drawn to the more-ness of life. Don't let that be a bad thing. It's OK to want more - in fact, it's amazing. It means you aren't settling. It's time to dig your heels in and take action.

I can think of a thousand times in my life when I should have and could have shown up but didn't. I let my belief that other things and people were more important than my dreams, but they weren't. I am important and my dreams are important.

Today you are going to commit. YOU WILL SHOW UP FOR YOURSELF.

Now, I know life happens, trust me, oh how I know, so I have created a way to let life happen and still show up. I'll share my secret with you. I give my life rules. For example, I host a call Monday to Friday EVERY WEEK, ALL YEAR LONG at 9 AM. As soon as I am on the call, I feel so crazily in my element. Before the call, it's a different story. Before the call, I come up with a dozen reasons not to show up that day. Everything from, I am so flipping tired to I have a mountain of work to do, to, I really should get out and exercise this morning.

Here's the thing, though, I have a rule. The only way I will EVER miss any kind of meeting is if I am physically too ill to show up, that means vomiting or in the hospital, OR, If one of my kids is physically ill and needs me to be there, OR, if there is a death in the family. Otherwise, there is no reason good enough for me not to be there.

If I can't sleep at night and stay up until 2 AM and look and feel like a bag of shit, I'm still showing up for that meeting. The rule stops me from getting in my way. I place these rules on EVERYTHING. Even relationships. If someone in my life causes me to feel anything less than amazing, the rule is, I remove them from my life by whatever means necessary.

I'm out to achieve the so-called impossible, so I need to be willing to protect my physical, mental, emotional, and environmental space to make sure I can achieve my goal.

What rules can you add to your life to protect you from your bad habits? Journal around this today and start implementing RULES RIGHT AWAY!

8

THINKING ABOUT CHANGING YOUR GOAL?

By now you've probably learned about how hard it can be to set some boundaries for yourself and others around achieving your impossible goal. You may already feel the, 'how long does it take' syndrome, and maybe you've thought about changing your goal.

DON'T - you CAN do this.

You haven't gotten there YET!

I want you to look at the word integrity.

We are going to start small here and build on this.

What is ONE thing you know you need to do for your goal?

- Is it accounting?
- Social media presence?
- Health-related?

Select one small thing you need to improve to move towards this goal. Just one goal such as going to bed at 9:00 p.m. instead of 10:00 p.m. so that you feel more rested. Hydrate more. Water is crucial for us to perform in the best way possible.

Once you have a new rule, stay in integrity with it ALL day. Do it for yourself and remind yourself that it's about stretching out and away from who you were and closer to who you need to be. When your mind wanders from what you promised yourself you would do, snap your mind back, and JUST GET IT DONE. Each time you get the 'am I there yet' feeling, come back to this practice.

This is how we build integrity and more importantly how we learn to trust ourselves.

9

HAVING IT ALL

When you get to that place where you have everything you ever dreamt of or thought you could or SHOULD have, things feel incredible. When you reach the place where everything is working as you want it to, everything is amazing, and life feels incredible, don't you think you're going to like that? When the newest phone came out that you REALLY wanted, did you get it? Perhaps when you decided it was time to join Netflix, did you want that and get it?

These are real and honest questions. When you have everything you ever dreamt of or thought you could or SHOULD have, do you think you're going to like it?

Let's get real – if you freakin' wanted it, you WOULD already have it. It's that fucking simple. You can come up with a million silly excuses for why that's not true or it's because of this or that or the other thing, but no. It's not. EVERYTHING you've made non-negotiable in your life has happened.

. . .

Everything you decided you wanted, you took for yourself.

That's just how people work.

So, let me ask you again, although let's ask it in another way. Why do you NOT want to get there?

Just pause for a moment, tune in, and ask –

'Why would I NOT want to get rich, physically fit, fulfilled, loved and in love, fully supported, experiencing all of life and myself at its best (or whatever your goal is) ... why would that be bad or wrong or even not SAFE?'

It's an important question to ask because if you feel as though you MIGHT just be holding yourself back from accomplishing your impossible goal, and we both know what I'm about to say next, you aren't going to accomplish it.

When entrepreneurs start their impossible goal challenge, they don't yet realize that at the end of the day, they CAN just 'flick the switch' and decide to BE that next level version of you who you need to be. There isn't any REAL work to do. You just decide, be and then do.

It's that simple, and also there are indeed reasons we hold ourselves back from achieving what we want. Sometimes even for life! It's frustrating, even infuriating, to look back and see that day after day after day you had sabotaged yourself, or, worse, wondered 'what's wrong with me?'

All you had to do was claim it. You're here now, and today you can do this very thing.

Let's say you've got it going on in one or more areas of life, yet you continually fail to do what you promise yourself you will, or know that you should have it going on in another area. Then, it's time to decide who and how you want to be in that area, and just be it!

. . .

I have a solid history of doing exactly this. In my twenties, I was in great shape, but my money situation was shit, and also my EMOTIONAL health was, let's say, less than perfect, yet I was happy in my relationships! I had a GREAT lifestyle, lots of freedom, and flexibility. Just a little note on priorities, yes? We ALWAYS get what we highly value and make a must.

So –

My body was great, hell. I was hot.

My relationship was amazing.

My quality of life was great.

The money situation was a flipping awful mess.

And my emotional health was terrible – I never felt good enough for anyone deep down inside. As the years passed, I did the work on my money mindset and dug myself out of the $200k debt hole I'd created, eventually going so far as to become what I would say is a decent start to being wealthy.

Meanwhile, my relationship was getting undeniably worse and worse. It was toxic, to say the least.

My physicality started to fluctuate.

Lifestyle freedom was still on point, and only getting better.

Still, I was focusing on being stable with the growth of my wealth.

Money had sorted itself out a LOT and was continuing to get better and better and my lifestyle freedom and flexibility rocked. I was also, becoming more and more connected to purpose and truly doing what I was meant to be doing with my message.

I finally dealt with my health and that was huge.

I couldn't understand why my relationship was a raging fire most days. I didn't look at how I wanted my life to look, except for the odd occasion when I somehow flipped the switch for a minute and a half.

The thing is, I KNEW I could have it all. I just hadn't accepted that

I could have it all in all areas. For years now I've dug into the exact kind of work we're talking about here.

I asked myself questions about why I held certain things at arm's length ... why I would NOT want the outcome I said I wanted ... What would be bad or wrong or scary about getting to the place I dreamt of?

You see, I thought that in the time it would take me to work through my emotional stuff, I would lose what was once an amazing relationship. In hindsight, not taking the time to work on that stuff is what cost me my relationship.

I can laugh about how silly that was now, which I think is a good thing to do. It takes the POWER out of it by laughing and finding the humor in it. I also found that curiosity IS helpful.

Learning to understand the deeper resistance in the psyche, if for no other reason than that being the person who continually does this work, who looks inward, demands an answer, then SHIFTS that shit so that it will get you out of fear and into action.

The unapologetically extra badass who DOES in fact 'have it all.'

We are taught to look at why we want things but never to look at the other side of why we also don't want them.

What do we have to let go of to go where we want to go?

I simply got to a point where I decided ENOUGH WAS ENOUGH, I insisted on being happy as FUCK, no apology!

You too? Good!

10
CREATING CERTAINTY

Are you feeling it yet? Is that little voice inside your head saying, "You've got this".

I know for me, I still go back to my whiteboard and my pads of paper, trying to map out all of the crazy-ass scenarios that may help me achieve my impossible goal, and every time I do it, I just can't see HOW to make it all happen.

Then the doubt creeps in, and the more time passes, more of those little bits of doubt creep in, and a little more and a little more.

Is that happening to you? If not yet, I hate to tell you it will. I promised to be real and open with you on this journey, so let me hold to that. It will creep in, slowly like the sun setting at night, making everything gradually get darker and darker, and as this happens, your confidence begins to fade.

A question to ask yourself to help with this is, "What kind of certainty can you tap into when shit hits the fan?" Grounding points are EVERYTHING in business, and you need one. You need a grounding point to help you focus when that little voice comes in. For example, certainty for me is that I will always be able to get on a live call and teach with complete confidence, even if I didn't know how to create a social media post. I know how to do that, AND I know my audience loves it.

Certainty to me is that I will always have love because I am a mom with two beautiful kids and my life would NEVER be without love.

Certainty, for me, was knowing that when the whole world shut down due to Covid, I could still exercise without gym equipment. I could do sit-ups, crunches, and pushups, and I still had legs to run. Even though I couldn't go to the gym, I knew with certainty I could still exercise.

What does certainty look like to you? How can you create space to fall into when you have those moments of struggle?

Make a list and review it until it becomes your go-to list. Don't look externally for all the answers because we already have them within us.

11
THE MARKETING SIDE OF ACHIEVING YOUR GOAL

BE KNOWN FOR WHO YOU ARE AND WHAT YOU DO

This vastly overlooked sentence is EVERYTHING when it comes to your success. If people don't know who you are or what you do, that sucks from an ego standpoint. Furthermore, it means that they don't know if you can help them...now that's a REAL PROBLEM.

The key to successful authority marketing is good content, but what if you have little to no experience in marketing with content? Businesses can be built entirely on referrals or networking, after all. Adopting a system that generates leads using content is a daunting prospect.

Your content might not create enough leads to be sustainable. There are innumerable blogs out there so how do you get your ideal client or customer to read yours? Maybe your blog does attract readers, but that means nothing if your calls to action are ignored.

Are you sure your content is reaching your target audience? All the expertise in the world means nothing if it falls prey to obscurity. It's important to build your profile among the right people.

Today's lesson is the Authority Marketing Statement.

It looks like this:

I am an authority marketing expert helping coaches struggling with imposter syndrome hit 6 and 7 figures using authority marketing.

I am a ______.

I help_______.

So that they can ________.

By (doing what)_________.

This is the first thing I teach every single person I work with because they need this level of clarity. If sales aren't coming in, it almost always comes back to their true level of understanding of the authority marketing statement.

You don't just want to describe the perfect client, you want to attract them with friggin' ease. So talk to them.

Really open your mouth and say all the things you want to say yet don't, or my favorite, the things you think you can't say. Who says you can't say them? And is that person the rule maker of all rules?

NO!

So why the heck are you leaving your success to a supposed rule-maker whom you probably don't even know and, therefore, can't trust and shouldn't be listening to anyway!

You should be saying everything you want to say, the good, the bad, and the ugly because when you step into authority marketing it becomes EASIER.

The clients come easier.

The money comes easier.

Success comes easier.

That, my friends, is the real secret to achieving your impossible goal. Saying all the things you want to and need to today without holding back.

Most of you won't, and it's truly sad because the rest of us will be experiencing incredible lives exactly as we want them and on our own damn terms, and you'll still be wondering how we did it.

I just told you how we did it!

We stopped acting and started being.

It's so magical how quickly and easily we can have what we want. We just have to open up and claim it.

Stop hiding who you are.

Stop silencing yourself.

Stop pretending.

Stop making yourself smaller.

Stop trying to fit in.

Stop trying to say what you think they want you to say.

Stop trying to be perfect.

Just say the things you want to say. Say all the things, and don't hold back! Pause for a moment and get your authority marketing statement down on paper.

Was it easy to 'label' what you do? Did you have clarity on how you serve others and what they really get out of it at the end of the day, or, did the process feel a bit overwhelming?

You see, clarity is the ultimate key to success. No business owner can market themselves or their business if they don't know who or how they help people, and I see this ALL THE TIME!

Think about the last time you asked for help. Maybe you hired a coach, maybe you needed a VA (virtual assistant). Maybe you wanted marketing support. Perhaps it was that you signed up for some free training.

. . .

What types of things were you saying to them or yourself? Was it, "I am just so stressed I literally can't sleep at night?"

Maybe it sounded like, 'I am SO ready to take things to the next level but I have no idea how."

It's probably VERY likely that these are the same kinds of things your prospective clients are saying, and when you know how to spot them, you know that you have the right people in front of you.

Grab some paper and write down all the things that your perfect client would be saying, so that next time they come along, you know how to spot them.

12

CLEANING UP YOUR WORKSPACE

CLUTTER: transitive verb. : to fill or cover with scattered or disordered things that impede movement or reduce effectiveness, a room **cluttered** with toys. It makes perfect sense that when you are surrounded by clutter you are distracted.

Now I am not a fan of cleaning once a week. On Sunday's we do a deep dive of floors, countertops, and laundry, yet overall during the week, I do everything in my power to remove the clutter from my workspace, my mind, and my emotions every single day.

Here is what I want you to do: Take note of your mental clutter. Perhaps there are things on your 'to-do' list that have been coming up for weeks and you haven't done them. Take note that each time they come up they are interfering with your current task at hand.

Perhaps there are things that you are avoiding.

Your assignment is to tackle this list, part of it, all of it, or at the very least, SOME of it.

Start the decluttering process of your mental and emotional state. It's not easy. Truth be told, it just plain sucks while you are going through it. Just bite the bullet and do it!

Next, declutter your physical environment. I suggest starting with your wallet, your fridge, and your desk. Why do you ask? The first is where your wealth lives and breathes, the second is where your health experiences happen, and the third is where productivity is created. Ensuring that these three priority places are always neat and tidy will help you to create balance in your mind.

Trust me it works!

13

DO WHATEVER IS NECESSARY TO BRING YOUR IDEAS TO LIFE

One of the silliest things I've ever done is delay taking action on something I KNEW I wanted to do. Every single time I got off my keister and just did 'the thing', I've kicked myself for not just doing it sooner.

There are things we avoid because of fear and things we avoid because we don't truly understand their importance. Then some avoid it because they are just plain old, lazy.

The little ideas that pop into your head, those that make you go hmmm, that's a good idea, those are the ideas to act upon. Bring those ideas to fruition by taking action.

An idea may seem small and insignificant, yet trusting in yourself when that spark comes, and you drop what you are doing to take action, you'll be rewarded in a big way.

If every one of those little ideas doesn't get you the results you wanted, then it's the exact opposite. What you want is to achieve your impossible goal and by taking action, you come one more step closer to it.

So what's the one thing you're going to do in your business?

No matter what the results of this one thing are, I want you to celebrate it. Yep, take a quick moment to say thank goodness I did that. It's going to help you with the fail-forward mindset. You are training your mind to see the good so you can attract it. More good, so you can get over hurdles faster, so you can think, act, explore and MOVE ON.

This is a powerful lesson that will yield incredible results.

Let's celebrate the sh!t out of every lesson we've ever learned and thank the universe for getting us one step closer to our goals.

14
THE KICK IN THE ASS YOU NEED

If you've ever wondered what's been holding you back, I'm here to give you a slight kick in the ass and let you know there is ALWAYS only one answer to that, YOU.

You are the only and exact reason you are where you are.

Between your thoughts, actions, and behaviors, you've brought yourself here.

If your business isn't where you need it to be to make your impossible goal a reality, it's time to ***SAY THE THINGS! SAY ALL THE THINGS, NEVER STOP SAYING THE THINGS!***

The long and short of it is, the faster you tell your clients **your** truth, the faster you and they get results.

People don't want all the information you keep trying to give them; they want transformation!

They want to relate.

They want to RESONATE.

They want you to see them, understand them; in most cases, they want to know that YOU WERE ONCE THEM!

THAT'S IT. After 15 years of marketing, that IS the only secret that matters when it comes to success in marketing and all parts of the business.

Every day, show up and speak your unfiltered mind to your clients. Share the good, the bad, and the ugly. Be willing to 'get naked' with them because once they hire you, that's exactly what you'll need from them for transformation.

The real and the raw - the starting point at which they are, the ugliness of how they got there, and the rawness of what it's going to take to get them out of where they are and into where they want to be.

Your clients will almost ALWAYS come to you in their most vulnerable state, so stop throwing your list of videos that they will receive, jumping up and down about the number of calls you are going to have with them, or the AMAZING workbook you created when all you have to do is show them you understand them.

It's time to rip the freakin band-aid off and show them who you are.

What's real and raw about you? What are you REALLY feeling about life? Business?

Wealth? Goals? Time? Relationships?

Expose who you are. NOW! RIGHT now.

Stop reading, create a post, or an email, or a live video. Just do it, once you've ripped that bandaid off and said the things you REALLY think and feel, not only will you feel damn good and you will attract people who get lit up by what you have to say and they will be hooked!

15

A MINDSET HACK TO HELP YOU STRETCH

Run Into Pain! It sounds silly, right? It's worth it. One of the most valuable things I've learned along the way is to not be afraid of pain because the truth is there is no way to cut it out of your life completely. It shows up at the worst time and when we least expect it.

Most of the time we are unable to avoid it, yet what we can do is accept, embrace, and run straight at that shit, look it straight in the eyes, deal with it, and get on to something better.

Today is a reflection day. I want you to think about pain today, but not from a deep-rooted tragedy kind of way, rather from an understanding that the fear of embarrassment is pain.

Don't avoid doing things because you fear the pain of judgment.

Not showing up for yourself causes pain.

All of these things equate to a less happy, less joyful, less fulfilled life.

What have you been avoiding?

Now run...straight at it, and put everything you have into overcoming it.

All you have to do is believe and declare, and YOU CAN shift past it in moments. We always have a choice in how long we stay stuck in something.

Reflect, take action, overcome.

16

TIME

Time is on your side. Surely you're about to disagree in every way humanly possible, but the thing is, you're wrong! You've got 24 WHOLE hours a day. What are you doing with them?

When my clients fly off all the reasons why something didn't get done, can't get done, likely won't happen, probably won't work for them...I give them the kick in the butt they need. You see, there is your truth, and then there is THE truth. Let me explain with a very real story (side note, I can't say I am proud of this, but it's a great lesson).

Sarah is standing in line at her favorite cafe, wearing a fabulous outfit, and of course, dying for shoes - to help paint the picture. She's in a hurry to get to her next appointment. There are three people patiently waiting in line behind her, to order their morning cuppa joe.

Just as she grabs her latte from the barista's hand, she gets a bump from the gentleman standing in line behind her, and SPLASH, the coffee goes everywhere.

Sarah immediately, and hastily turns around and says, what the heck, didn't you see me? She steps aside, scoffs at him, and walks towards a table, where she sees a pile of napkins.

Later on, she gets a call from her dear friend Alex, who says hey, I saw you at the cafe this morning. Saw the spill, but thank goodness that little old lady didn't fall over.

HUH? Sarah thinks to herself.

Didn't you see the jerk who spilled my coffee all over me?

"Sarah, there was a little old lady behind him, and she was standing in line, looking a little pale. I think she was lightheaded because she tipped forward and grabbed onto the man behind you. Sucks because as he turned around to help her, your purse hit him as you grabbed your latte. Luckily, he steadied that lady. Didn't you see that?"

While I was acting like Queen B!T@H, some little old lady almost fell over and it was my purse that hit him. I mean, did I REALLY need a purse that was more like the size of carry-on luggage? My truth was VERY different than the truth, and I was ultimately the real reason why my coffee spilled.

Your time management is A LOT like this. Your perception of it is very different from its reality. When we choose to live in our truth instead of THE truth, we are often limited. I see clients doing this all the time.

- I'm too busy.
- I won't have time to get it done.
- I didn't start soon enough, so I may as well not start.
- It'll cost too much to do it in that amount of time.
- I know you are thinking like a badass rebel, or maybe a high and mighty king, I want you to digest the following list of reasons why you could FEEL like you are too busy.
- You can feel or be too busy if:
- You don't manage your time well.
- You try to do everything on your own.
- You focus on the wrong things.
- You continuously add new and unimportant things to your plate.

17

MANAGING YOUR TIME TO SUPPORT YOUR IMPOSSIBLE GOAL

The first step is to give yourself time. You have to be willing to take the time to make the time. When I think of saving time, what I do is figure out how to save energy and the time piece happens on its own.

If you had more energy, what could you accomplish towards your impossible goal this week? This month? This year?

For me, saving energy means I don't do anything I don't want to do. Could you, a-freakin-imagine what life would be like if you only did the things you wanted to do - if you were A LOT more selfish about your goal instead of a little or not at all. Just think though, if your possibly impossible goal were lived out, how would you feel? What would your life be like?

After year 3 of doing my impossible goal challenge, it became abundantly clear that time was NOT on my side. In a matter of 3-days, I was able to change that, not just for the year I worked on that goal then, and I will for the rest of my life.

I set up pre-order groceries, carpooled the kids to school, automated banking, hired 2 VA's, hired someone to clean and do laundry weekly, taught my kids a 10-minute end-of-day tidy routine, gave my son a $20 a week allowance to take out the garbage and mow the lawn.

I stopped saying yes to everyone, stopped feeling guilty about it, and everything started to get easier because I was using less energy and I had more time.

"But I don't have the money to do all that, Sarah." I didn't either, but I found it. I did the things that felt impossible. I gave up some of what I thought I needed (I now see I really didn't NEED things like cable and the best phone plan).

- Order Groceries online = $10/week in delivery fee
- Carpooling = this one saved me money
- Automated Banking = this one saved me money too because everything was paid on time and I saved BIG TIME on interest fees and late payment charges.
- VA Services = $400/month
- House Cleaning = $60/week
- Tidy Routine = NOT a penny, but both of my kids are now amazing cleaners.
- Allowance for my Son = $20/week

Total: $760 per month

I was no longer exhausted every day, my son learned the value of work, and I had over 15-hours a week back. Let's average this out of cost vs. value. If I had my lowest sales volume and sold one of my lowest coaching packages a week I cover this. This means I have 15 hours to work on closing ONE client. My lowest package is $25,000. I'd make $100,000 a month and it would cost me $760 to do this.

I'm sure you've heard these kinds of scenarios before, and I get that it can still be scary to take these kinds of leaps, especially when you feel like you have little or nothing to give. Scary or not, it's necessary. Even if you just implemented one each month, think of how much energy you'd have and how open your days would be to do what matters; becoming the person you need to become to achieve your impossible goal.

There will officially be no more complaining that time is not on your side because it is. You just aren't utilizing it.

Time to get to work and make some adjustments.

18
MONEY TALK

I just shared one amazing hack on how to create more wealth, and I can't resist diving deeper into this. Some will say that if you get me talking about creating wealth, you will likely never shut me up. To date, that has been wildly true.

Money is a HUGE obstacle for people, and I am sure you would agree. Money could inevitably be one of the things that you feel is going to prevent you from achieving your impossible goal. I'm here to tell you, that's not an option.

First things first, if you haven't read Have it All, by Moi, please pop back into Amazon and grab your copy. You'll invest $15 and make a buttload more than that. It's a 30-day money mindset book that features daily action steps you can do to physically create more wealth.

Next, remember your ONE AND ONLY rule; you cannot change your impossible goal in any way. There is no reason to say, I can't achieve it, Sarah, because I need __ amount of money.

Find it.

Make it.

Borrow it.
Manifest it.
Ask for it.
Increase your prices.
Create a new product.
Get a job.

Remember, this is about doing what it takes to get to where you want to go.

It's about stretching, growing, and becoming someone different, not because you aren't good enough as you are, but because the possibilities out there are endless for you and we're about to prove it this year.

Money is easy to create. List the money mindset beliefs you have that are holding you back. The keyword to tune into is *belief*. You can change your beliefs in the blink of an eye by simply choosing to believe something is different and acting accordingly.

Having money is as simple as deciding to have money. Deciding that wealth is who you are, creates that shift. Not who you will be, but who you are.

If the money isn't coming, say to yourself, the money isn't here YET. This tells your brain it IS coming in time. Don't allow yourself for one moment, or one second to be less than wealthy. No matter what your current state is, declaring wealth will not be something that holds you back and it will be so damn easy to you now, you'll wonder why you stressed about it before.

A NOTE FROM ME

As I embark on a new year and a new **Impossible Goal Challenge**, I've set my goal that by the age of 40, I want to be on the Forbes list of wealthiest women in the world. This is my impossible goal for 2022!

How will I make this happen? I have NO clue! Am I close to making this happen? I'm about as close as a frog is to flying. Do I believe I can do it, not a chance yet I'm certainly willing to give it everything I've got.

As I previously mentioned, my goal last year was to live a world-class life while having both of my businesses earn $300,000 a month, and while some months have felt world-class, some months felt as though I was rehashing every trauma that I ever experienced. Those are necessary evils I moved through.

The challenges that held me back allowed me to find true peace within myself. I feel it is an important part of creating a world-class life.

I ended up closing one of my businesses this year, and that put a HUGE damper on my plans. I remember the day I sent an internal email that I was closing and no one in my audience knew because I was embarrassed.

I felt like a complete failure, and my real, raw truth is that the business WAS a failure. It drained me of every ounce of time, energy, money, and peace of mind.

This year I restructured everything, from start to finish, and I'm excited to say that in January I will re-launch. This time PROPERLY with all the right people and all the right pieces.

Equipped to earn well over $300k per month, I couldn't be more proud. The shame that I once felt wasn't necessary. I've learned this year that part of living a world-class life means letting go.

I let go of a lot to make this impossible goal possible.

I left a 3-year long relationship that I was desperate to be in that was holding me back from being happy...REALLY, REALLY, REALLY happy. At times I thought I was happy, yet I wasn't really, REALLY, happy.

I have so much love in my life now that it's crazy incredible and it too, feels world-class.

I let go of shame, guilt, fear, and pride, and it wasn't easy. However, in doing so, I became free to be me, flaws and all.

Oh, I spent money where I shouldn't have and then, made more to do the things I needed to, and along the way, I learned there is always more money where that came from and I can have what I want, and what I need.

Here's what I did:

- Fired clients who drove me crazy.
- Published 3 books plus the one that I'm writing right now.
- Co-authored 2 books.

- Launched my clothing line.
- Invested in over 17 properties.
- Started a savings fund to launch my retreat center.
- Created new friends and lost a few.
- Lost my brother to drugs.
- Lost my best friend to cancer.
- Lost my 5-year old niece to illness.
- Made peace with some of my family.
- Learned how to love the good, the bad, and the ugly.

Through all of that, life went on, and I just was. I didn't let anything stop me. I decided what I wanted for me, my life, my dreams, my legacy, my family, my heart, my health, and all these were most important. I have one life and I don't have to live it fully, but I get to. It's a choice.

I don't know what the next 365 days hold for you yet I imagine if you stick with this, if you truly push yourself to become the person who can achieve your impossible goal, you will go on the most amazing adventure you've experienced yet.

I know this year I did just that.

I am sending each and every one of you, man or woman, so much love and such good vibes. I believe you have it in you.

Sarah xx

THANK YOU

Leave a Review

If this book has provided you with insight, tools, stories or thoughts you'd like to share, please leave an honest review on Amazon or Goodreads Your reviews help prospective readers decide if this is right for them & it is the greatest kindness you can offer the author.

Thank you in advance.

ALSO BY SARAH QUINN: HAVE IT ALL

Have It All - Step up, Let Success Flow. 30-Day Money Mindset For Coaches

Book #1 Quit Fucking Around Series

Get Your Copy Here

www.amazon.com/Sarah-Quinn/e/B095M85574

A Sneak Peek Inside

You get to be wealthy because you decide you deserve it.

Sunday afternoons have always been about one thing for me; dreaming about how wealthy people lived.

I would walk through houses that started in the low millions and drive cars that had more fancy tech than the electronic store. I certainly couldn't afford any of it then yet, I damn sure knew I loved being around it. I'm sure one can agree that it was wrong to waste the realtor's time pretending I could afford a home.

I'd later go home and dream of having a similar life and this was my first taste into what money could buy, and I loved it. I loved the stainless steel in the kitchen, the 20+ acres of beautiful land, and the smell of the leather seats in the shiny new car.

I wanted to experience all of it every day.

For the next 10 very long years, I worked 12-14 hour days, and guess what? I got nowhere fast.

Sure I made money yet, it always seemed to go out as fast as it came in. I worked harder and longer and then, I hit burnout.

Maybe you've been there, and if you haven't let me tell you, true burnout leaves you feeling paralyzed and so exhausted you can't do a thing at that point. I dropped all the fancy balls I was juggling in the air and I couldn't even balance my work.

The money took on a whole new face then. Forget the car and the mansion.

How the hell was I going to pay my bills? Feed my kids? Cover car insurance? I didn't have enough to get by let alone keep dreaming big.

That was that. All of my dreams vanished along with my belief that I could have it all.

I couldn't figure out what I did wrong. I mean, I worked my friggin ass off, took all the classes, read personal development books weekly, and went on retreats. You name it and I, I did it.

Now, years later, know why it didn't do a damn thing towards me becoming wealthy.

Working harder is NOT the answer to having wealth.

But Sarah, so and so says...

No, my dear, they are wrong.

Hard work can be part of creating wealth but it is not the answer to having, keeping, attracting, and sustaining wealth, and in most cases, hard work is the exception - not the rule.

The rule is -> you get to be wealthy because you decide you deserve it.

END OF STORY.

Maybe you picked up this book because you know me or, perhaps you are brand new to me. If you do not know me yet, I am the founder of The Savvy Networker Global, now open in 36 cities supporting business owners from every walk of life, in various stages of their journey, and some with the worst money mindset I have ever experienced. That's why I felt compelled to write this book.

You see, together with running a global company, I also work with bad-ass coaches who are ready to be the authority figure in their industry. What does this mean? They have to freakin LOVE making money because achieving success with authority marketing means money flows with more ease, higher amounts, and more frequently.

I thought to myself, this can't be the best-kept secret for my high ticket clients, so I started to spread the message of money mindset to all 15000 entrepreneurs I work with. The result... I'll let you know how it goes in a later book.

For now, what I can say is everyone who's taken my course has shown major growth in their business and personal wealth. How far they will take it? You will have to wait and see.

Over the next 30 days, you are going to learn how to treat money so that you can get it, use it, replenish it, and keep it.

Here is the phrase I want you to start using every time you let go of a single penny, *"There is always more where that came from!"*

Remember that you are a friggin bad-ass wealthy babe, and money flows into you like those cupcakes you tried to avoid eating last week.

Don't worry girl, I was right there with you!

Money is all around you, and as long as you treat it right, it will continue to be yours in amounts far greater than you have ever imagined.

If you are feeling broke as fuck right now, it's because you have a bad relationship with money. We'll get to that a little later on in the book. For now, it's time to start adopting a healthy money mindset.

You deserve to be wealthy as fuck!

You deserve to feel good about money.

You deserve to have all the money you can imagine and more.

You deserve to spend money on whatever you like without feeling guilty.

You deserve to be debt-free.

You deserve to be financially secure.

And now, my beautiful new friend, let's get you there.

The thing you have to understand about money is that you get to decide the level at which you play.

Do you want to be rich, wealthy, and healthy? Now you need to get your ass up there, stand tall and live that sexy ass life you want.

Yep, you heard me, each time you want to claim something such as wealth, health, career, location, whatever it is you dream of, climb your ass up there and just decide it's where you belong.

No one can take it away from you except you. Ultimately you get to decide what you deserve in this life. If you've been short on wishes coming true, it's time to dive into what you believe you deserve because, YOU DESERVE IT ALL, and then some.

This book was developed as a support tool for ***100 Journal Prompts for Ready to Be 6 and 7 Figure coaches*** (applicable for any type of business owner).

What I have come to learn over the years is that money comes easily to me

ALWAYS. And it's not because I work 24/7 or because I give up things to have it. It's because I know without a doubt it's coming. I trust this and the world delivers.

I want the same thing for you so that you live in the truth that money is easy to attract, and that the world will always give you more than what you need as long as you ask for it and believe in what you ask for it.

The next 30 days are all about taking your existing mindset and tossing it out the window. I like to call it *quantum leaping success* - going from where you are to a dramatic shift into something new and different, something better than you imagined.

Before you ask yourself what the secret is to achieve this, I will tell you. It's so simple you may want to chuck this book out the window. Don't do that because that very same thought process IS what is holding you back. You believe it has to be hard, and it doesn't.

I'm not saying think it into existence. I'm saying you can just decide to be wealthy, have it all, and make the most out of the life you've been given. Sure, you may have to get your hands dirty some days but it would be boring if you didn't have.

You may even have to call that creditor you've been ignoring or fill out that paperwork that's hiding in the bottom of your drawer but, this is part of having it all while doing the work AND trusting FULLY that the world will give you EVERYTHING you need.

So let's get to work, you gorgeous wealthy woman. Wealth is all around you and we are going to use the next 30 days together to bring it into existence.

I suggest grabbing a journal and journaling each day. Even if it's a one-liner, just jot down a wealth statement. I've added a few in the back of the book to get you going.

100-DAY JOURNAL PROMPTS FOR READY TO BE 6 & 7 FIGURE COACHES

Book #2 Quit Fucking Around Series

Get Your Copy Here

www.amazon.com/Sarah-Quinn/e/B095M85574

A Sneak Peek Inside

Rolling out of bed, I stretched my arms up high toward the sky. With my flowy white pajama pants and gold sparkle PJ top wrapped around me, I looked out the window and thought to myself, *"Holy shit, this is everything I ever dreamed of. I fucking did it, and didn't I prove all the haters wrong!"*

My bare feet felt good on the floor as I walked over to brush my teeth and then step onto the yoga mat. My yoga room soaked in the smell of tangerine and mint with the sun beaming in was spectacular. Again, I thought to myself, *"Wow, I've created an amazing life."*

As I stepped off of the yoga mat, sipping a hot cup of matcha, I reached for my journal and my favorite gold color pen. There it was, a moment that took place every single day as my religion. The sacred moment, never to be interrupted, never to be ignored, and most importantly, never to be rushed. It was time to journal.

Words pour out of me daily that sometimes feel as though they make ZERO sense. Heck, I'm sure most of it didn't make sense, but the things that DID make sense, holy shit, those things were magic.

When my pen hit the paper everything became real. It's always been as though I connect to my soul or my higher power if you will.

My journal is the one place I knew I could be completely raw, without fear, always. I could be anything I wanted to be on those pages and at the same time, I could be everything I didn't want to be because no one was reading but me.

I dreamed BIG.

I let myself get wild and crazy.

I let myself get downright angry.

I worked out my frustration.

I strategized my business.

I even dreamed of love.

My journaling isn't just about writing though. After each and every session, it is a sacred practice where I close my eyes and visualize what I had created on those pages, what I want to let go of in life, and what I desire. Day after day, I notice that these things begin to come into my life with ease, l with flipping ease. Do you know how incredible that feeling is?

Since I am always about sharing my truths, I had no friggin clue what ease felt like. In fact, at first, it was so foreign to me, it felt REALLY uncomfortable. I was always waiting for the other shoe to drop, and so I began journaling about what life would look like if the shoe didn't drop and if my life just kept moving forward in the most amazing ways.

That's exactly what happened. It moved forward, and it was fucking amazing. Wait, it IS fucking amazing.

I encourage you to create your own journaling ritual. Think of it as a recipe. What do you need to make it good?

Candles?

Natural light?

Complete quiet?

Music?

Essential Oils?

A special space in your home?

Whatever it may be, make it yours and make sure it feels good for you. Journaling is just as much about the process as it is the outcome.

You will see what I mean as you continue through the next 100 days.

In the Journal I ask you a question or create a prompt that you answer in written form in your copy of The Journal.

Sounds pretty simple, doesn't it?

Here's the thing, if any question makes you feel like you do NOT want to answer it, take a serious look at WHY NOT. It's a sure sign you need to do some work.

I want you to look for questions that trigger you or make you feel resistance toward them. In my opinion, investigating those questions with depth will help you have a better and more meaningful transformation.

Book #3 Quit Fucking Around Series

Get Your Copy Here

www.amazon.com/Sarah-Quinn/e/B095M85574

A Sneak Peek Inside

The Very Public Break Up

As in public debates where sellers break up their audience, the goal with authority marketing is to bring TOGETHER like-minded prospects (we'll get into this later when we get into philosophical marketing).

When you post debatable content, you become the referee between a divided community.

I want to flick people in the forehead when I see this because it's one of the worst things you can do. You may as well post: "Hey Joe, meet Samantha here in my network. She is 100% for vaccines and you are 100% against them...please buy my course."

Joe and Samantha are too busy foaming at the mouth while they battle out who's right and who's wrong about vaccines, hopefully in a private chat. Let's be real, this very public debate is likely happening right on your Facebook wall for everyone to see and engage with.

"But I am so passionate about X, Sarah!

GREAT! I'm passionate about the way the hot married guy down the hall looks, and I don't jump his bones just because I'm passionate.

I'm about to start WW3 with wifey if I do this, and how am I going to feel every time I walk out of my condo?

Some of you have taken what authenticity is supposed to be and turned it into the #1 reason you have ZERO clients, and yes, I understand what freedom of speech is, and Luv, you can speak freely. However; beware. There are consequences and they impact the top 3 things that get impacted with one of them being your sales.

Unless your job is to sell people on the fact that they should/shouldn't get vaccinated, do you really NEED to post your opinion on this?

By removing these four things from your social feeds, AND social conversations, you leave room for what really matters to your audience; education, connection, and conversation.

Get Your Copy Here

ABOUT THE AUTHOR

Sarah Quinn is an entrepreneur and writer, real estate investor and officially has her own clothing line. Sarah is based in Quebec City, Canada. When she isn't furiously unleashing her true message via Facebook Lives or her podcast, A Poor Coaches Guide to A Rich Life (https://anchor.fm/apoorcoachesguide), she is running her online coaching business as an entertainer, speaker, and success mentor to coaches around the globe.

With a new series of books, more than a decade in online business, and several hundred products and event launches under her belt, Sarah is known as a Content Queen who just doesn't stop. She believes that you CAN have it all on your terms, as long as you're willing to get honest with yourself about what you're here to do in the world.

Her mission is to help coaches learn to use their voice as a powerful tool to inspire themselves and others to lead with authenticity, creating a life wilder than their wildest dreams.

Sarah is also a mom of 2 and is obsessed with teaching her children that you can have it all, exactly as you want and on your terms.

Sarah is also an expert in "No B.S" coaching and would love to help you create a business you love, completely on your terms!

Follow Sarah here:

facebook.com/coachesmakingmoney

ABOUT RED THREAD PUBLISHING

Stories Change Lives

We believe in the power of women's voices & stories to change the world. We support women not only to write & publish their books but to own their voice, accelerate empowerment & reach global impact. Because women matter.

Do you have a story that must be told?

Sierra Melcher, author & founder of @RedThreadPublishing, & our team will support you every step of the way.

Redthreadbooks.com & info@redthreadbooks.com

ALSO BY RED THREAD PUBLISHING

The Anatomy of a Book

Available on Amazon & everywhere books are sold.

This book brings together the tools & wisdom from publishers, book marketers, professional podcasters & public speaking coaches to teach you how to make the most of launching & selling your books, skills & services. An invaluable guide and addition to your author library.

Made in the USA
Coppell, TX
05 November 2026

11301603R00049